Hidden Bugs

Contents

Food hunt   2

What is hidden?   4

Hidden wings   8

Thorn bugs   10

Bugs that mimic   12

Glossary and index   20

Can you spot the hidden bugs?   22

Written by Isabel Thomas

Collins

Food hunt

Gardens, parks and forests look **tranquil**. But they are full of animals on the hunt for food!

Animals love to
snack on bugs!

What is hidden?

Some bugs lurk in dark spots to keep out of sight.

But some bugs are hidden in plain sight!

stick insect

A good trick is to look like part of a tree.
This moth looks like bark.

This moth **larva** looks like a twig.

larva

twig

Hidden wings

Green wings are hard to
spot on a shrub or tree.

Wings that seem to curl are hard to spot in the forest.

Thorn bugs

This bug clings to trees with thorns.
It looks like a thorn itself!

To feed, thorn bugs suck
sap from trees.

Bugs that mimic

Meet the bug with a larva that tricks bees!

They form a troop and march up stems.
They **mimic** a bee.

larva

When a bee visits, the bugs dart on to its back.

The bee zooms to its nest.

The bugs march in and slurp the food.

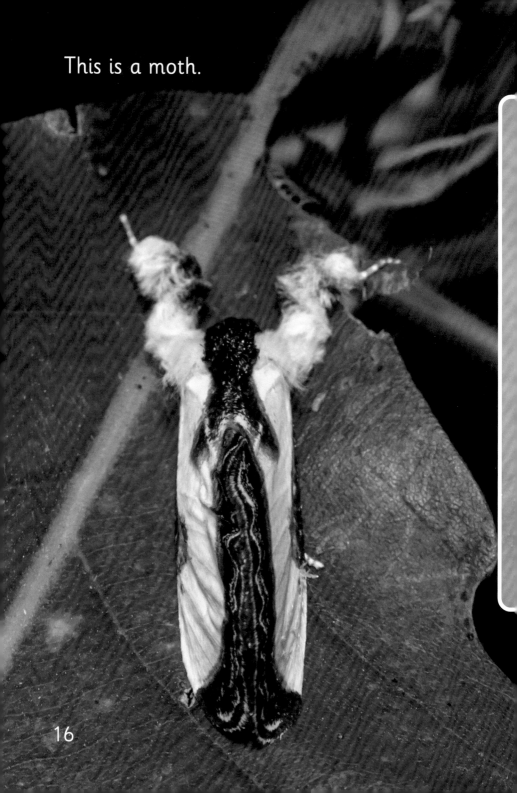

This is a moth.

This is a larva.

They look like dung! This is a smart plan
not to be seen as food. Yuck!

Look out for the hidden bugs that lurk in gardens and parks.

Keep back and do not **disturb** them!
Bugs do important jobs for us.

Glossary

disturb upset or mess up

larva an insect grub

mimic look like a different thing

tranquil still, as if resting

Index

bee 12–13, 14–15

larva 7, 12–13, 17

moth 6–7, 16

thorn bugs 10–11

wings 8–9

Can you spot the hidden bugs?

After reading

Letters and Sounds: Phases 3 and 4

Word count: 227

Focus phonemes: /ch/ /sh/ /th/ /ng/ /ai/ /ee/ /igh/ /oo/ /oo/ /ar/ /or/ /ur/, and adjacent consonants

Common exception words: of, to, the, full, are, you, they, like, do, some, when, out, what, love, be

Curriculum links: Science: Living things and their habitats; Animals, including humans

National Curriculum learning objectives: Reading/word reading: read accurately by blending sounds in unfamiliar words containing GPCs that have been taught; read other words of more than one syllable that contain taught GPCs; Reading/comprehension (KS2): understand what they read, in books they can read independently, by checking that the text makes sense to them, discussing their understanding and explaining the meaning of words in context; identifying main ideas drawn from more than one paragraph and summarising these

Developing fluency

- Take turns to read a page, encouraging your child to read sentences ending in an exclamation mark with a tone of surprise.
- Your child could imagine they are reading to a younger child, so need to read expressively to hold their interest.

Phonic practice

- Practise reading words with adjacent consonants and long vowel sounds:
  plain   trees   troop   slurp   smart
- Ask your child to read the following words with more than one syllable and adjacent consonants:
  page 2: tranquil page 2: forests page 19: important page 19: disturb

Extending vocabulary

- Look together at the glossary on page 20. Discuss new glossary definitions for the following:
  page 3: snack on (e.g. *eat little bits*)   page 4: lurk (e.g. *hide*)
  page 9: curl (e.g. *roll up*)
- Check the definitions work in context.